THE VISIONS & SIGNS OF
Ezekiel

His Eminence Metropolitan Youssef
Translated by St. Mary and St. Demiana Convent

ST MARY & MOSES ABBEY PRESS

CONTENTS

Introduction

"God, who at various times and in various ways spoke in time past to the fathers by the prophets, has in these last days spoken to us by His Son, whom He has appointed heir of all things, through whom also He made the worlds." (Hebrews 1:1–2)

God spoke through the prophets, and Ezekiel is no exception. In this book, we will cover the five visions granted to Ezekiel and expound on their intended meaning. All these visions have a beautiful meaning and all are Messianic—about the Messiah—helping us understand the economy of salvation. We will also give a bird's-eye-view of the signs in the life of Ezekiel.

We would like to extend our deepest thanks to all who joyfully labored in the translation process, to bring this English translation to light; may the Lord reward them with the heavenly in place of the earthly.

May God accompany the reader on the journey through this book, and open our hearts to learn from these visions and signs and their intended meaning.

Metropolitan Youssef
St. Mary and St. Demiana Convent
January 7, 2025
Nativity Feast

Chapter 1

Historical Setting of the Book of Ezekiel

In the name of the Father, and of the Son, and of the Holy Spirit, one God. Amen.

We are going to study the book of Ezekiel, especially the visions and symbols.

We will begin with a general overview of the book of Ezekiel, and then examine Ezekiel's life as a person, and as a prophet. Without this introduction, neither the wonderful visions described nor the significance of the signs presented in this book would be fully understood.

We know very little about Ezekiel the prophet. We know he was the son of Buzi and that he was born in the year 623 BC. He was a priest of the descendants of Zadok. Some Jewish rabbis posit that Buzi was Jeremiah the prophet—the Jews, belittling him, nicknamed him Buzi. This opinion claims that Ezekiel is the son of Prophet Jeremiah. This is one [outlandish] opinion, in case you come across it.

The time of Ezekiel the Prophet was characterized by two factors that affected and shaped his life. The first is the reformation by Josiah the king in 621 BC, two years after the birth of Ezekiel. The second was the presence of several other prophets, including Jeremiah. Ezekiel was to become a priest, following in his father's footsteps. Ezekiel's strong connection to the temple suggests that he may have witnessed its restoration and that he created many memories therein. Unearthing the lost books of the Law jolted King Josiah's joyful zeal, propelling him to hold a great celebration, likely leaving a lasting impression on young Ezekiel.

The priests' housing was located on the eastern wall of the temple, and since Ezekiel was the son of a priest, it is safe to assume he was living there. Notably, the school designated for the sons of priests was in this same area; we could imagine him playing in the yard around his school and the temple—creating memories and forming a deep attachment. As the son of a priest, he may have assisted, for example, by lighting the candles or the censor. As he grew, he probably sat with the teachers in the temple, asking questions and listening to their teachings, just as we read in the New Testament that Christ, at the age of 12, went to the temple and sat with the teachers to learn from them. With Josiah's restoration of the temple, Ezekiel was certainly looking forward to the day he would reach the age of 30 and serve the Lord as a priest.

As mentioned earlier, Ezekiel was likely affected by earlier prophets such as Amos, Hosea, Isaiah, and Micah. For instance, if we were to compare the prophecies in Ezekiel and Hosea, we find many similarities, as if Hosea's influence was deeply imprinted on Ezekiel. This era was marked by a prophetic revival, with many prophets contemporary to Ezekiel emerging, including Jeremiah, Daniel, Nahum, Zephaniah, Habakkuk, and Obadiah.

In reading Ezekiel, it is clear he was influenced by the words of the prophet Habakkuk, but it was the prophet Jeremiah who left the deepest impression on him. Jeremiah witnessed the reformation by King Josiah, which impacted the building [of the temple], the sacrifices, the Ark of the Covenant, the law, and circumcision—yet unfortunately left the people's hearts unchanged. Thus, Ezekiel's message crystallized in this promise: "I will give you a new heart and put a new spirit within you; I will take the heart of stone out of your flesh and give you a heart of flesh" (Ezekiel 36:26). Ezekiel did not focus on restoring the temple from the outside (the building), the Ark of the Covenant, etc., but rather on the human heart—believing that reformation starts from within, through a new heart and a new spirit. These two factors influenced Ezekiel's upbringing and prophetic mission.

During this time, there were also political events that affected Ezekiel the prophet. The most pivotal event was the demise of Nineveh, the capital of the Assyrian empire, when Ezekiel was about 10 years old. At the age of 15, the Pharaoh of Egypt took his army and occupied Palestine; King Josiah tried to support Assyria against Egypt, so the Pharaoh killed him.

At 16, Ezekiel witnessed the death of King Josiah and the corruptness of his successors. The death of Josiah marked the end of a 14-year era of peaceful reformation. Following Josiah's death, Jehoahaz, his youngest son, was anointed king but he sat on the throne for only three months. Because he was very wicked, those three months were prolonged in the eyes of the people. At that time, Jeremiah warned the people to return to God.

9

Jehoahaz was taken captive to Egypt, and the Pharaoh appointed his brother Jehoiakim as the new king. The Pharaoh of Egypt, occupying Israel and Palestine, did not want to destroy Jerusalem for two reasons: its tax-paying inhabitants provided him with revenue; and with the fall of the Assyrian empire, the Babylonian empire had begun its rise. Pharaoh, wanting Egypt to become the next great empire, decided to maintain good relations with the kingdom of Judah to form a coalition with them against Babylon.

Ezekiel was about 16–20 years old when he observed these events. Egypt sent idols to Jerusalem; he started seeing the priests and the educators begin to worship the idols, meanwhile the service in the temple gradually deteriorated. He witnessed Jeremiah the prophet, growing older, rebuke the priests with zeal. While sitting in the temple, Ezekiel might have listened to Baruch the scribe reading from the prophecies of Jeremiah to the people.

At that time, a copy of the prophecy of Jeremiah was sent to the king of Judah, to incite him to return from his evil actions and idol worship. The king, furious, tore the prophecy, burned it, and tortured Jeremiah. (Jeremiah was the prophet most tortured by the kings of Judah.) Ezekiel, full of zeal and love for God, was disturbed by what was happening around him and felt bitter. He began revolting within his heart against the religious leaders, sensing their corruption. Knowing that if he mentioned Jeremiah, he would be ostracized, Ezekiel never mentioned him by name, although he was greatly influenced by his writings.

Thereafter, Nebuchadnezzar, the king of Babylon, gained victory over the Pharaoh of Egypt; Pharaoh's dream of Egypt becoming the next great empire dissipated, while Babylon began gaining strength. When the king of Judah, Jehoiakim (who was allied with the Pharaoh against Babylon) saw that Nebuchadnezzar defeated the Pharaoh, he pledged loyalty to Nebuchadnezzar and to Babylon.

Babylon besieged the kingdom of Israel prior to besieging the kingdom of Judah. Although most inhabitants of Judah wanted to be allied with Egypt, not Babylon (because they witnessed the destruction of the kingdom of Israel at the hands of Nebuchadnezzar), the king of Judah made a pact with Nebuchadnezzar because he had the upper hand.

When Ezekiel the prophet was about 23 years old, Jehoiakim rebelled against Babylon's authority over him. As a result, Babylon besieged Jerusalem for two years. During this, Jehoiakim died, perhaps killed, and his son Jehoiachin ascended to the throne, ultimately surrendering to Babylon (Ezekiel was about 25 years old by that time). It is worth mentioning that the destruction of Jerusalem by Nebuchadnezzar did not begin immediately after the surrender of Jehoiachin. The captivity occurred in two stages. During the first captivity, Nebuchadnezzar treated the kingdom of Judah gently—he did not destroy the city or the temple, but only took the king captive to Babylon along with all the gold and silver of the temple.

Having been raised in the temple, Ezekiel was familiar with all its gold and silver articles. One can imagine Ezekiel's feelings when he found all the cherished temple contents he had grown up with taken to Babylon; the gold was melted and carried away. Following Jehoiachin's reign, his evil brother Zedekiah ascended to the throne. Zedekiah defiled the temple and allowed idol worshippers to worship inside the temple. All this greatly affected Ezekiel.

Nebuchadnezzar took all the strong educated youth from Jerusalem (to avoid any revolutions against Babylon), and left the illiterate destitute people in Jerusalem. This was during the first stage of the captivity of the kingdom of Judah. During this stage, God did not allow the destruction of Jerusalem or the temple, in order to give the inhabitants of Jerusalem an opportunity to repent. Despite the prophecies of Jeremiah and Ezekiel, the people mistakenly believed their captivity would be short-lived, expecting to return soon. Rather than taking this opportunity to repent, their wickedness multiplied.

Ezekiel was taken into exile at the age of 25. In Babylon, there was a river (originating from the Euphrates River) called Chebar. While in exile, Ezekiel purchased a house near this river and lived in it; he was trying to signal to his compatriots that the exile was going to last a long time (not a year or two as they assumed) and he kept pleading with them to repent. He lived in a city called Tel Aviv (different from the current Tel Aviv in Israel). After he wed, his wife, whom he loved very much, died, but he received divine instructions not to lament her publicly but to sigh within his heart (Ezekiel 24:16). This was the only time Ezekiel expressed his own feelings about a personal issue.

Ancient tradition says Ezekiel's place by the river is where Noah lived and also the location of the Garden of Eden. There are several references in the writings of Ezekiel to Noah and to the Garden of Eden, for example: Ezekiel 14:14, 20; 28:13; 31:8, 9, 16, 18; 36:35 and more.

When Ezekiel was exiled to Babylon at the age of about 25, he realized that he was going to spend the rest of his life in captivity in Babylon with the rest of the captives from Judah. Initially, he silently observed and meditated on the events occurring to his people, keeping everything to himself, while bitter in his heart. He read the prophecies and knew what events lay ahead; he was especially attached to the prophecies of Jeremiah. At the time, Babylon was extremely powerful, which caused a state of depression and despair for all the Israelites. They wondered how they could rebel against such a great kingdom as Babylon. Simultaneously, they anticipated a quick return, since Nebuchadnezzar had not *yet* destroyed Jerusalem or the temple. However, as their exile prolonged, they began to lose hope because of the might of the Babylonion empire.

Nebuchadnezzar did not place any restrictions on the civil or religious rights of the Jews brought into captivity. He allowed them their own meetings to gather for prayer, and allowed the elders of the Israelites to be their judges. He also allowed them to trade and to own houses and possessions, even though they were captives. This allowed Ezekiel the prophet to buy a house wherein he lived. They were also able to communicate freely with the Israelites in Jerusalem. In fact, they were allowed to send and receive mail from Jerusalem. Although they had all these privileges, they were depressed because they were away from their country and away from the temple.

When Ezekiel was 29 years old, four years into captivity, King Zedekiah came from Jerusalem to visit Babylon and received a warm welcome. After a year, when Ezekiel was 30, King Zedekiah came again to visit Babylon, but this time Nebuchadnezzar had changed and started to destroy Jerusalem and the temple. This caused great grief in the heart of Ezekiel the prophet.

Ezekiel's visions began 5 years into his exile, when he was 30 years old (the age when he could practice as a priest). He saw the beautiful first vision mentioned in the first chapter of his book, when the heavens were opened to him, and he saw Almighty God on the throne and the four incorporeal creatures.

God had sent him to prophesy to the Israelites, marking the beginning of his prophetic mission, a journey that would span 22 years (from age 30 to 52).

During Ezekiel's fourth year of exile, King Zedekiah came to visit King Nebuchadnezzar in order to build positive relations. In the fifth year of his exile, King Nebuchadnezzar started destroying Jerusalem and the temple. In the sixth year of exile, King Zedekiah tried to side with the Pharaoh of Egypt against Babylon and King Nebuchadnezzar. Ezekiel did not like the pact between King Zedekiah and the Pharaoh of Egypt. He rebuked the king, asserting that a Jewish king who believes in God, who swore an oath with Nebuchadnezzar, should not break the covenant he made—even if it was with a pagan king (Ezekiel 17:18). Ezekiel told him that if he breaks the oath, he will fall under divine punishment; if he united with the Pharaoh, his destiny will be like King Jehoahaz who was removed by the Pharaoh, and like Jehoiakim who was taken to Babylon. Ezekiel also told King Zedekiah that Jerusalem and the temple would suffer the same fate as that of Samaria (the kingdom of Israel)— which had been destroyed and whose inhabitants were taken to exile. Jerusalem was destroyed and laid waste in the eleventh year of Ezekiel's exile.

In the eighth year of his exile, Ezekiel was 33 years old, and a new pharaoh ruled over Egypt—different from the one who had made a pact with Zedekiah in the sixth year. This new Pharaoh encouraged King Zedekiah to rebel against Babylon. After attempting rebellion, Zedekiah tried to flee at night, but the Babylonians arrested him in Jericho, killed all his sons in front of him, plucked out his eyes, and brought him bound to Babylon. Ezekiel prophesied the exact date when all this would take place (24:2). After arresting Zedekiah, Nebuchadnezzar left Jerusalem in ruins, destroying every part of the city and the temple. The Israelites began to flee to Egypt, and they took with them the aged Jeremiah and Baruch the prophets for protection, although both prophets did not want to leave Jerusalem.

The countries surrounding Judah rejoiced at the calamity befalling the kingdom of Judah. God hates such gloating, so He revealed prophecies to Ezekiel against those neighbors and then punished those neighboring countries for their actions.

With all these sad events, one can imagine the sorrow in Ezekiel's heart, yet he did not lose hope—hope such as we read of in Chapter 34, verse 13. What helped Ezekiel cling onto hope was that God revealed to him a very beautiful vision—the New Jerusalem, the new temple, and the new worship—in the last chapters of the book of Ezekiel. Due to the vision, Ezekiel was reassured that all who are in exile would return to Jerusalem, despite the stature of King Nebuchadnezzar, and despite Jehoiakim's imprisonment.

There is a beautiful vision that we read every Hosanna Sunday during the General Funeral that refers to the general resurrection but also bears another meaning. God took Ezekiel, showed him a valley of bones, and asked him if there is a chance for these bones to live. When He asked him to prophesy to the bones, Ezekiel noticed that flesh started to form on the bones, followed by nerves and being covered with skin. Next, He told him to prophesy to the spirit. When Ezekiel prophesied, the spirit came from the four winds, entered the bodies, and raised up a great army.

The meaning of this vision is that God can bring up the Israelites as He raised up these bones; they can be liberated from exile and restored to Jerusalem. Ezekiel never lost hope that the Israelites would go back victorious, realizing that God allowed for the exile as an opportunity for them to repent. This is why Ezekiel wrote chapter 36—if we repent, God will forgive our sins. God will unify the Northern Kingdom (Israel) and the Southern Kingdom (Judah); they were all united in the kingdom of Christ, along with the Gentiles who believed: "A kingdom, a priesthood," as we say in the fraction prayer for the Apostles. God will forgive our sins if we repent (Ezekiel 36).

Ezekiel also assured the Jewish people that God would condemn the selfish shepherds and priests—that He Himself would be the Shepherd of the people, as we read in Ezekiel 34.

Ezekiel also prophesied about the Messianic era, in the words of Christ: "I will give you a new heart and put a new spirit within you; I will take the heart of stone out of your flesh and give you a heart of flesh"—the work of the Holy Spirit, which was fulfilled by the incarnation of Jesus Christ (Ezekiel 36:26). In this way, humans would be liberated from their captivity to sin (the exile to Babylon is symbolic of captivity to the devil and sins).

The final chapters in the book of Ezekiel, which speak of the temple in heaven, are very beautiful, especially when read in conjunction with the book of Revelation.

Unfortunately, despite the many talents of Ezekiel the prophet, he did not have a great impact on the people. Ezekiel was a priest, poet, and prophet; he had some wonderful attributes. People came to enjoy listening to him as a form of entertainment, but they never followed his advice, as we read in Ezekiel 33. He did not have a powerful impact on his contemporaries; rather, they hated him because he exposed their evil acts. He always referred to Israel as the rebellious house, to the point that God once told him, "Indeed you are to them as a very lovely song of one who has a pleasant voice and can play well on an instrument; for they hear your words, but they do not do them. And when this comes to pass—surely it [the prophecy] will come—then they will know that a prophet has been among them" (Ezekiel 33:32–33), but it will be too late.

They loved the world and sin more than God; hardheartedness came from their pride and ego, their beloved sin, or their love of money—the three temptations on the mount, as St. John reiterates: "All that is in the world—the lust of the flesh, the lust of the eyes, and the pride of life" (1 John 2:16). This is true captivity. The priests and the religious leaders were very proud; they could not tolerate someone rebuking them. As a result, their resentment grew towards Ezekiel. Reportedly, one of the judges of Israel killed him because Ezekiel had reproved the judge for idol worship.

Ezekiel was buried in Shem's tomb, according to St. Epiphanius. During the days of St. John Chrysostom, they relocated his relics to Constantine (modern-day Turkey). St. John Chrysostom gave a great sermon on Ezekiel the prophet on that occasion. We celebrate his departure, or his martyrdom, on the 5th of Parmoute. Ezekiel's life is beautiful and contains many lessons for us, which we will cover when we look at his signs and visions. This was an overview of Ezekiel's life, his environment, and what impacted him.

Chapter 2

A Bird's-eye View of the Signs
in the Book of Ezekiel

The book of Ezekiel is rich with signs and symbols. Here we will give a bird's-eye view of the signs in the book of Ezekiel. A *sign* refers to an incident or event yet to occur, conveyed through symbolic imagery.

For instance, consider the story of the two eagles in Ezekiel:

> And the word of the Lord came to me, saying, "Son of man, pose a riddle, and speak a parable to the house of Israel, and say, 'Thus says the Lord God: "A great eagle [Nebuchadnezzar] with large wings and long pinions, full of feathers of various colors, came to Lebanon and took from the cedar the highest branch. He cropped off its topmost young twig [Jehoiachin] and carried it to a land of trade; he set it in a city of merchants. Then he took some of the seed of the land and planted it in a fertile field; he placed it by abundant waters and set it like a willow tree. And it grew and became a spreading vine of

low stature; its branches turned toward him, but its roots were under it. So it became a vine, brought forth branches, and put forth shoots. But there was another great eagle [Pharaoh] with large wings and many feathers; and behold, this vine [Zedekiah] bent its roots toward him, and stretched its branches toward him, from the garden terrace where it had been planted, that he might water it. It was planted in good soil by many waters, to bring forth branches, bear fruit, and become a majestic vine."' Say, 'Thus says the Lord God: "Will it thrive? Will he not pull up its roots, cut off its fruit, and leave it to wither? All of its spring leaves will wither, and no great power or many people will be needed to pluck it up by its roots. Behold, it is planted, Will it thrive? Will it not utterly wither when the east wind touches it? It will wither in the garden terrace where it grew."'" (Ezekiel 17:1–10)

When we come to exegesis, we find those two eagles referring to Nebuchadnezzar and the Pharaoh of Egypt. Nebuchadnezzar is the first great eagle, and the branch from the cedar of Lebanon refers to Jehoiachin who was taken to exile in Babylon. This sign, which appears in the book of Ezekiel, is explained later in the same chapter.

Moreover the word of the Lord came to me, saying, "Say now to the rebellious house: 'Do you not know what these things mean?' Tell them, 'Indeed the king of Babylon [Nebuchadnezzar the eagle] went to Jerusalem and took its king [Jehoiachin] and princes, and led them with him

> to Babylon. And he took the king's offspring, made a covenant with him, and put him under oath. He also took away the mighty of the land, that the kingdom [Jerusalem] might be brought low and not lift itself up, but that by keeping his covenant it might stand.'" (Ezekiel 17:11–14)

Nebuchadnezzar took the best and strongest among the youth to Babylon and left the weak and the uneducated in Jerusalem so they could not rebel against Nebuchadnezzar. This is the interpretation of verse 14. He took the strongest (the topmost young twig) to Babylon, a city of merchants. The strong ones settled by the "abundant waters," the River Chebar. "Low stature" means it is constrained, unable to rebel against the king of Babylon. "Its branches turned toward him" means they made a pact with Nebuchadnezzar.

When Zedekiah tried to make a pact with the Pharaoh of Egypt, Ezekiel warned Zedekiah that although he was mistaken in making a covenant with a pagan king (Nebuchadnezzar), he should not break the covenant or abandon him.

> But he rebelled against him by sending his ambassadors to Egypt, that they might give him horses and many people. Will he prosper? Will he who does such things escape? Can he break a covenant and still be delivered? "As I live," says the Lord God, "surely in the place where the king dwells who made him king, whose oath he despised and whose covenant he broke— with him in the midst of Babylon he shall die." (Ezekiel 17:15–16)

Here God explained by asking, "'Will he prosper' after breaking the covenant?" Surely he will not! As persons consecrated to God, as Christians, are we committed to our covenant? If the one who broke a covenant with a *pagan* king will not escape punishment, how much more so people who break a covenant with God? Zedekiah, who vowed to King Nebuchadnezzar of Babylon and broke that covenant, shall die in the midst of Babylon.

> Nor will Pharaoh with his mighty army and great company do anything in the war, when they heap up a siege mound and build a wall to cut off many persons. Since he despised the oath by breaking the covenant, and in fact gave his hand and still did all these things, he shall not escape. (Ezekiel 17:17–18)

Ezekiel was forewarning Zedekiah of the Pharaoh's inability to help. This is referring back to the symbolism in verse 7 where he talks about the other eagle (pharaoh). This vine (the kingdom of Judah) bent its root toward the Pharaoh of Egypt and stretched its branches toward him (after it had been bent toward Nebuchadnezzar). It is currently planted in good soil (Nebuchadnezzar) but is now trying to reach out to the Pharaoh of Egypt. Will it thrive? No, you (Zedekiah) will not—if you are going to make a covenant with the Pharaoh against Nebuchadnezzar, you will not succeed and that will lead to you (Zedekiah) being uprooted and withering. Pharaoh will not be able to help you (Zedekiah) with many people or with great power. The kingdom of Judah is planted, but it will wither.

There are three types of signs:

1 - Enacted signs

2 - Visual signs

3 - Personified signs

Since Ezekiel used a plethora of signs, some commentators called him "The father of symbolism." Though others used signs before him, Ezekiel used signs more than anyone. Isaiah used signs; so did Jeremiah, such as when he went to the house of a potter and smashed a pitcher in front of the people as a sign of the destruction of the city and its people (Jeremiah 18).

1) Enacted signs

Signs in the book of Ezekiel are of three types. One type of sign is where a story has an underlying meaning, later explained to the people. There are signs that are enacted signs done by Ezekiel before the people. Take for example Ezekiel 37:

> As for you, son of man, take a stick for yourself and write on it: "For Judah and for the children of Israel, his companions.' Then take another stick and write on it, 'For Joseph, the stick of Ephraim, and for all the house of Israel, his companions." Then join them one to another for yourself into one stick, and they will become one in your hand. (Ezekiel 37:16–17)

God told Ezekiel to take a stick and label it for the kingdom of Judah and those from the kingdom of Israel who are companions to the kingdom of Judah, and to label the second stick for the kingdom of Israel and the other tribes who are companions to the kingdom of Israel. Then to take the two sticks and join them together to become one stick in his hand. When he did this in front of the people, they asked him to explain his actions.

> And when the children of your people speak to you, saying, "Will you not show us what you mean by these?" —say to them, "Thus says the Lord God: 'Surely I will take the stick of Joseph, which is in the hand of Ephraim, and the tribes of Israel, his companions; and I will join them with it, with the stick of Judah, and make them one stick, and they will be one in My hand.'" And the sticks on which you write will be in your hand before their eyes. (Ezekiel 37:16–17)

This is a sign for the future conjoining of the kingdom of Israel and the kingdom of Judah to become one kingdom—this is an example of enacted signs.

2) Visual Signs

There are also visual signs. For example, Ezekiel prophesied to the dry bones (a prophecy read during the General Funeral) as mentioned in Ezekiel 37. This was a sign that God will raise up the children of Israel and return them to Jerusalem. God gave Ezekiel a visual sign:

> The hand of the Lord came upon me and brought me out in the Spirit of the Lord, and set me down in the midst of the valley; and it

was full of bones. Then He caused me to pass by them all around, and behold, there were very many in the open valley; and indeed they were very dry. And He said to me, "Son of man, can these bones live?" So I answered, "O Lord God, You know." Again He said to me, "Prophesy to these bones, and say to them, 'O dry bones, hear the word of the Lord! "Thus says the Lord God to these bones: 'Surely I will cause breath to enter into you, and you shall live. I will put sinews on you and bring flesh upon you, cover you with skin and put breath in you; and you shall live. Then you shall know that I am the Lord.'"'" So I prophesied as I was commanded; and as I prophesied, there was a noise, and suddenly a rattling; and the bones came together, bone to bone. (Ezekiel 37:1–7)

Surrounded by so many dry bones, God asked Ezekiel to prophesy to the bones. As Ezekiel prophesied, there was a noise and a sudden rattling; the skull gravitated towards the vertebral column, the ribs began collecting, the arm bones came together, and the leg bones with the hip joint approached and attached to form a complete skeleton. Next, the nerves, muscles, flesh, and even the skin covered the skeleton, so that it looked like a dead body, but it did not have a spirit.

Indeed, as I looked, the sinews and the flesh came upon them, and the skin covered them over; but there was no breath in them. Also He said to me, "Prophesy to the breath, prophesy, son of man, and say to the breath, 'Thus says the Lord God: "Come from the four winds, O

> breath, and breathe on these slain, that they
> may live."'" So I prophesied as He commanded
> me, and breath came into them, and they lived,
> and stood upon their feet, an exceedingly
> great army. Then He said to me, "Son of man,
> these bones are the whole house of Israel. They
> indeed say, 'Our bones are dry, our hope is lost,
> and we ourselves are cut off!'" (Ezekiel 37:8–11)

As we said, we read this in the General Funeral prayer; it is a prophecy about the final Resurrection. The house of Israel considered themselves dry bones; depressed, they lost all hope. Exiled, they considered themselves dead, similar to the dry bones. Why does he say, "Son of man, these bones are the whole house of Israel?" Because during the period of captivity they reached a bare-bone state of despair.

> Therefore prophesy and say to them, "Thus
> says the Lord God: 'Behold, O My people, I will
> open your graves and cause you to come up
> from your graves, and bring you into the land of
> Israel. Then you shall know that I am the Lord,
> when I have opened your graves, O My people,
> and brought you up from your graves. I will put
> My Spirit in you, and you shall live, and I will
> place you in your own land. Then you shall know
> that I, the Lord, have spoken it and performed
> it,' says the Lord." (Ezekiel 37:12–14)

Here the *graves* are symbolic of exile. This is also a prophecy about the New Testament; those in exile represent the righteous ones in hades. Our Lord Jesus Christ went down to those in exile (hades) and restored them to paradise. This is also about the resurrection from the dead on the last day.

When did these events take place? Did this sign actually happen? No, most likely not. This was a prophecy, a vision. It bore more than one meaning. *Historically* it meant the children of Israel would return from exile. It also referred to the descent into Hades to restore Adam and his children to paradise. *Spiritually* it meant we, whom Satan exiled to death by sin, would enter into the holy life. In verse 14, "I will put My Spirit in you" refers to the Holy Spirit received in the sacrament of chrismation. This also refers to the church in the New Testament. As I said, this is a vision, because no actual resurrection occurred; he saw a vision and we call this a visual sign.

Another such sign was the taking of the measurements of the New Jerusalem and its temple:

> He took me there, and behold, there was a man whose appearance was like the appearance of bronze. He had a line of flax and a measuring rod in his hand, and he stood in the gateway. And the man said to me, "Son of man, look with your eyes and hear with your ears, and fix your mind on everything I show you; for you were brought here so that I might show them to you. Declare to the house of Israel everything you see." (Ezekiel 40:3–4)

He described the measurements of the New Jerusalem and many of its meanings. The angel told Ezekiel to observe these and to declare what he sees to the house of Israel. Obviously all the measurements and descriptions symbolically relate to the return of people from exile and the renewed temple construction. It also refers to the New Testament church and to heaven.

3) Personified Signs

Amazingly, God used *Ezekiel himself as a sign*—this happened frequently. As Isaac was a sign for Christ when Abraham took him to offer him as a sacrifice, likewise Ezekiel played the role of the children of Israel in many situations. Take for example Ezekiel 12:

> "Therefore, son of man, prepare your belongings for captivity, and go into captivity by day in their sight. You shall go from your place into captivity to another place in their sight. It may be that they will consider, though they are a rebellious house. By day you shall bring out your belongings in their sight, as though going into captivity; and at evening you shall go in their sight, like those who go into captivity. Dig through the wall in their sight, and carry your belongings out through it. In their sight you shall bear them on your shoulders and carry them out at twilight; you shall cover your face, so that you cannot see the ground, for I have made you a sign to the house of Israel." So I did as I was commanded. I brought out my belongings by day, as though going into captivity, and at evening I dug through the wall with my hand. I brought them out at twilight, and I bore them on my shoulder in their sight. (Ezekiel 12:3–7)

God told Ezekiel to gather everything he would need as if going into captivity. Ezekiel played the role of the children of Israel journeying into exile. During the day, he gathered his belongings in front of the people, and during the night, he made as if he wanted to escape. God told Ezekiel to dig through the wall as one trying to escape. Who is the one who wanted to escape? King Zedekiah. God told Ezekiel to cover his face so that he could not see the ground; Zedekiah's eyes were blinded when he was taken to exile. Thus, Ezekiel was playing out the role of the children of Israel. God made Ezekiel a sign for the house of Israel. The people could not accept that they would be going into captivity, so God made Ezekiel into a sign for them.

God repeats this command to Ezekiel:

> Say, "I am a sign to you. As I have done, so shall it be done to them; they shall be carried away into captivity." And the prince [Zedekiah] who is among them shall bear his belongings on his shoulder at twilight and go out. They shall dig through the wall to carry them out through it. He shall cover his face, so that he cannot see the ground with his eyes. I will also spread My net over him, and he shall be caught in My snare. I will bring him to Babylon, to the land of the Chaldeans; yet he shall not see it, though he shall die there. I will scatter to every wind all who are around him to help him, and all his troops; and I will draw out the sword after them. (Ezekiel 12:11–14)

Here Ezekiel acted by taking his belongings and leaving during the daytime as if leaving Jerusalem, just to tell the house of Israel what is coming to them; what I did to myself will happen to you. He repeats here that Zedekiah cannot see the ground, because Nebuchadnezzar will put out his eyes.

In another place, God told Ezekiel:

> You also, son of man, take a clay tablet and lay it before you, and portray on it a city, Jerusalem. Lay siege against it, build a siege wall against it, and heap up a mound against it; set camps against it also, and place battering rams against it all around. Moreover take for yourself an iron plate, and set it as an iron wall between you and the city. Set your face against it, and it shall be besieged, and you shall lay siege against it. This will be a sign to the house of Israel. (Ezekiel 4:1–3)

Take a clay tablet and draw Jerusalem, then lay siege against it. This intimates that Ezekiel was an artist who could draw. Ezekiel was not just a prophet; he was a priest, a prophet, a shepherd, an administrator, a poet, a musician, an artist, a visionary (he saw many visions), and a theologian. He introduced many new theological concepts, especially about God giving us a new heart and a new spirit, and removing the heart of stone. He also talked about New Jerusalem. Ezekiel is a multi-talented beautiful personality. Ezekiel Chapter 1 is beautiful; we will cover it in our next chapter. Here, God ordered Ezekiel to draw the city and surround it, to declare to the people that Jerusalem will be besieged; God allowed this because they defiled the temple by introducing idols into it. God abandoned them to be besieged—Jerusalem would fall and its inhabitants would go into exile. Here God explained in detail what would happen.

A second prophecy follows:

> Lie also on your left side, and lay the iniquity of the house of Israel upon it. According to the number of the days that you lie on it, you shall bear their iniquity. For I have laid on you the

years of their iniquity, according to the number of the days, three hundred and ninety days; so you shall bear the iniquity of the house of Israel. And when you have completed them, lie again on your right side; then you shall bear the iniquity of the house of Judah forty days. I have laid on you a day for each year. Therefore you shall set your face toward the siege of Jerusalem; your arm shall be uncovered, and you shall prophesy against it. And surely I will restrain you so that you cannot turn from one side to another till you have ended the days of your siege. (Ezekiel 4:4–8)

God asked Ezekiel to lie on his left side 390 days (for the house of Israel), then on his right side 40 days (for the house of Judah). God laid on him a day for each year; the forty days are a symbol of 40 years. Contemplating on the number of these days, the Church Fathers said the sins of the house of Israel are the left-sided plagues such as the sins of murder, theft, deceit, and adultery, while the forty days are the right-sided plagues such as the sins of self-righteousness, self-esteem, the love of praise, and dignity.

So, what do the 390 days represent? The besiege of Jerusalem lasted 18 months as we read in Jeremiah Chapter 52. Then, when the army of the Pharaoh drew near besieged Jerusalem, the besiegers withdrew for five months; that means the city was besieged for 13 months (18 months minus five). Thirteen months are equivalent to 390 days. And the 40 days represent 40 years. Here, Ezekiel is himself a sign.

Yes, these siege days were upon Jerusalem, yet, as when he made the two sticks into one, there were people from the kingdom of Israel mixed in with the people of the kingdom of Judah in Jerusalem at this time. It is not exclusive that those are the sins of Israel and these are the sins of Judah. The right side always means power and a blessing; Jesus came from the tribe of Judah—that was the right side. The sum of the 40 and 390 days represents the sins of both the kingdoms of Israel and Judah. Church Fathers also contemplated: one observing the sun rising from the east has the north on the left side and the south on the right side—the kingdom of Judah was in the south and the kingdom of Israel was in the north.

There is another interpretation for the 390 days as a sign for the separate kingdoms of Israel and of Judah. The 390 days signify the duration of the separation between the two kingdoms at the hands of Jeroboam the son of Nebat. He effected this separation during the reign of Rehoboam the son of Solomon in 975 BC, while the destruction of Jerusalem was in the year 586 BC. If we subtract 586 from 975 we will find the duration of the separation from the time of Jeroboam the son of Nebat until the destruction of Jerusalem is 390 years. This is concerning the kingdom of Israel.

There is also another interpretation for the 40 years. If it is 390 years since the kingdom split until the destruction of Jerusalem, there were 40 years from the death of the godly king Josiah (who introduced reformation) until the burning of Jerusalem. Although there had been sins and abominations in Jerusalem beforehand, they never reached the magnitude of the sins of Israel. Israel absolutely did not worship God, while Judah still had the laws, the temple, and the sacrifices. After Josiah died, however, they were filled with abominations, therefore God delivered them into exile.

If the entire duration is correlated to the siege, we need to remember that the siege occurred in two stages. The first stage was 390 days (13 months), followed by a period of withdrawal by the army of Babylon when the Pharaoh of Egypt came. Then the second siege lasted 40 days (God told Ezekiel to sleep on his side 40 days) until they entered the city and burned it.

Another sign:

> Also take for yourself wheat, barley, beans, lentils, millet, and spelt; put them into one vessel, and make bread of them for yourself. During the number of days that you lie on your side, three hundred and ninety days, you shall eat it. And your food which you eat shall be by weight, twenty shekels a day; from time to time you shall eat it. You shall also drink water by measure, one-sixth of a hin; from time to time you shall drink. And you shall eat it as barley cakes; and bake it using fuel of human waste in their sight. (Ezekiel 4:9–12)

God was declaring that during the siege around the city, there will be famine and people will eat food lacking nutrition. Each one's ration of food will be by weight and the water they drink will be by measure—revealing the state of famine of the people during this time period. God told him to use human waste for fuel to signify the defilement and impurity of the people—the siege occurred because of the people's extent of defilement and impurity.

> Then the Lord said, "So shall the children of Israel eat their defiled bread among the Gentiles, where I will drive them." So I said, "Ah, Lord

God! Indeed I have never defiled myself from my youth till now; I have never eaten what died of itself or was torn by beasts, nor has abominable flesh ever come into my mouth." Then He said to me, "See, I am giving you cow dung instead of human waste, and you shall prepare your bread over it." Moreover He said to me, "Son of man, surely I will cut off the supply of bread in Jerusalem; they shall eat bread by weight and with anxiety, and shall drink water by measure and with dread, that they may lack bread and water, and be dismayed with one another, and waste away because of their iniquity." (Ezekiel 4:13–17)

Ezekiel asked God to pardon him from "using fuel of human waste," so God allowed him to use cow dung instead. In fact, until today, in the poor villages in Upper Egypt they use cow dung (known as gella) as fuel for the oven to bake bread instead of using firewood. We have now seen examples of God using even Ezekiel himself as a sign to the people of the house of Israel.

Chapter 3

First Vision

In truth, Ezekiel saw more than one vision, perhaps five in all. The most exquisite vision is the one mentioned in the first chapter of the book of Ezekiel. The scenery of this vision varies from the scenery in the Book of Revelation. One needs to use the imagination to visualize it; some iconographers have attempted to depict it. We will try to simplify it; let us try to imagine it:

> Then I looked, and behold, a whirlwind was coming out of the north, a great cloud with raging fire engulfing itself; and brightness was all around it and radiating out of its midst like the color of amber, out of the midst of the fire. (Ezekiel 1:4)

The whirlwind gives us the feeling of the presence of God, similar to the "rushing mighty wind" experienced at Pentecost (Acts 2:2). The whirlwind means God's work is beginning to manifest and be declared.

He also saw a cloud, which signifies the approach of God, as we read in Psalm 104:3: "Who makes the clouds His chariot"; in Jeremiah 4:13: "Behold, he shall come up like clouds, and his chariots like a whirlwind"; in Nahum 1:3: "The clouds are the dust of His feet"; and in Revelation 1:7: "Behold, He is coming with clouds, and every eye will see Him."

He is unveiled in the fire. The fire is the same one Moses saw atop Mount Sinai, when the mountain was "burning with fire" (Deuteronomy 5:23). St. Paul spoke of Christ "revealed from heaven with His mighty angels, in flaming fire" (2 Thessalonians 1:7–8). The "fire engulfing itself; and brightness was all around it" indicates the might of God. Nothing can withstand fire; fire destroys everything in its path. Who can withstand God!

This fire with "the color of amber, out of the midst of the fire" was not a spark that ignites in straw and then dies out, nor was it the type that smelts metals. Despite this fire, the "color of amber" is present; the amber represents the steadiness of God; amber is the most fire-resistant of all metals. This metal is symbolic of the clarity and purity of the divine nature because it contains no impurities.

> Also from within it came the likeness of four living creatures. And this was their appearance: they had the likeness of a man. (Ezekiel 1:5)

We say in our hymns, God "who sits upon the cherubim"; these four creatures are the throne of God and carry the throne of God. They have a human anatomical appearance: body, legs, and head.

> Each one had four faces, and each one had four wings. Their legs were straight, and the soles of

their feet were like the soles of calves' feet. They sparkled like the color of burnished bronze. (Ezekiel 1:6–7)

We always say the four creatures each have a specific face: one like a human, one like a lion, one like an eagle, and one like an ox, but note that here Ezekiel says each one has four faces. It also says here that each has four wings, while in the Divine Liturgy we say each one has six wings; we will explain this shortly. They have large calves' feet (stability) because these are the ones carrying the throne of God. Again, the burnished bronze is a sign of steadfastness and purity.

The hands of a man were under their wings on their four sides; and each of the four had faces and wings. (Ezekiel 1:8)

Human hands are found underneath the two wings they use to fly (two wings to cover the body and two wings to fly), and the faces and wings are on the four sides.

Their wings touched one another. The creatures did not turn when they went, but each one went straight forward. As for the likeness of their faces, each had the face of a man; each of the four had the face of a lion on the right side, each of the four had the face of an ox on the left side, and each of the four had the face of an eagle. (Ezekiel 1:9–10)

The outstretched wing of one overlaps the outstretched wing of the one adjacent and so on, linking all the creatures. Since they have four faces, seeing in every direction, they need not turn when they move. Each one of the creatures has the faces of a man, a lion, an ox, and an eagle.

Before we move on, let us recap, so we can get a clearer visual. Four incorporeal creatures carry the throne of God. Each one is anatomically like a human being, having a head, body, arms, and legs. Each one has four wings—two wings are extended to connect the four with each other. Their feet are like calves' feet, symbolizing their stability. There is a human hand under each extended wing, and the other set of wings cover their body. Each creature's head has four faces, not only one face: lion and human on the right side, and on the left side an eagle and ox. This is why, with their four faces, when they move, they do not turn around because they can see in every direction.

The lion symbolizes God the king; the ox, God the sacrifice; the eagle, God the divine; and the human, the incarnation in the flesh. These are symbolic of the hypostasis of God the Son. Do these attributes apply to the Holy Trinity? Yes! The lion represents God's might, the ox represents God's patience and fairness, the human represents God's work and goodness, and the eagle represents God's magnificence and wisdom.

During the month of Koiahk, we chant of "the four living creatures around the throne of God pleading on our behalf." They intercede for all creation; the lion intercedes for the wild animals, the ox for domestic animals, the man for humanity, and the eagle for the birds. Since each creature has the four figures, the four intercede for our human race.

The four creatures are also symbolic of the four evangelists. The man (human) is symbolic for Matthew who wrote about Jesus, the Son of Man; the lion for Mark who wrote about Christ the King; the ox for Luke who wrote about Christ the Redeemer; and the eagle for John who wrote about Christ, the Son of God.

We also said the four creatures are symbolic of Christ Himself. The man represents the incarnation; the eagle represents His divinity and His ascension to heaven; the lion represents His courage to proclaim the truth and His resurrection from death; and the ox represents the priesthood of Christ as the redeemer and high priest who offered Himself as a sacrifice.

Searching Scripture, one would find varying visions based on the message God wants to deliver; John the Visionary saw a variation, Isaiah saw another, Moses saw yet another, and even Ezekiel saw two variations. Perhaps the most comprehensive vision is in Ezekiel Chapter 1. Comparing our current verse (1:10) with Ezekiel's second vision (10:14): "Each one had four faces: the first face was the face of a cherub," we find him seeing the face of a cherub (instead of an ox). There He told the angel to take a coal of fire (of God's wrath), and when Ezekiel attempted to intercede, the Lord would not have mercy; there is no sacrifice, no forgiveness—Christ the Redeemer—so no face of an ox. The cherubim are one rank, and the seraphim are another; the incorporeal beings who carry the throne of God are of the cherubim, as we say in our hymns: "He who sits upon the cherubim."

> Thus were their faces. Their wings stretched upward; two wings of each one touched one another, and two covered their bodies. And each one went straight forward; they went wherever the spirit wanted to go, and they did not turn when they went. As for the likeness of the living creatures, their appearance was like burning coals of fire, like the appearance of torches going back and forth among the living creatures. The fire was bright, and out of the fire

went lightning. And the living creatures ran back and forth, in appearance like a flash of lightning. (Ezekiel 1:11–14)

Seraph means fire. The burning coals of fire represent zeal. The flash of lightning represents God's mercy; lightning accompanies the rainbow—the covenant between God and man. So, they "ran back and forth, in appearance like a flash of lightning," meaning they are continually declaring God's mercy.

Now as I looked at the living creatures, behold, a wheel was on the earth beside each living creature with its four faces. The appearance of the wheels and their workings was like the color of beryl, and all four had the same likeness. The appearance of their workings was, as it were, a wheel in the middle of a wheel. When they moved, they went toward any one of four directions; they did not turn aside when they went. (Ezekiel 1:15–17)

Let us look at the wheel. It is composed of two frames within each other, perpendicular to one another. This configuration allows the wheel to move to the front or back, left or right. Had the wheel been configured from one frame, it would not have been possible to move in all four directions. It is not a small wheel but rather a massive one in size!

As for their rims, they were so high they were awesome; and their rims were full of eyes, all around the four of them. When the living creatures went, the wheels went beside them; and when the living creatures were lifted up from the earth, the wheels were lifted. (Ezekiel

1:18–19)

There is a wheel next to each creature. When the creature moves, the wheel moves along with it; if it rises, the wheel also rises with it.

> Wherever the spirit wanted to go, they went, because there the spirit went; and the wheels were lifted together with them, for the spirit of the living creatures was in the wheels. When those went, these went; when those stood, these stood; and when those were lifted up from the earth, the wheels were lifted up together with them, for the spirit of the living creatures was in the wheels. (Ezekiel 1:20–21)

The spirit of the creature is in the wheel, so if the wheel moves forward, the creature moves forward; if it moves back, the creature will move back also. If the wheel rises or stops, the creature does the same.

> The likeness of the firmament above the heads of the living creatures was like the color of an awesome crystal, stretched out over their heads. (Ezekiel 1:22)

The *firmament* consists of the two wings used to cover their face, forming the shape of a dome. Each has a total of six wings: two cover their face, two cover their legs, and with two they fly!

> And under the firmament their wings spread out straight, one toward another. Each one had two which covered one side, and each one had two which covered the other side of the body.

(Ezekiel 1:23)

Let us recap to help visualize. The two wings covering the face form a dome, and under that dome each creature's wing is stretched out toward the other creature from each side—there is a man's hand underneath these wings—and two wings cover their bodies. Each has the feet of calves. Next to each creature is a wheel circumscribed in another wheel, and the spirit of the creature is in the wheel.

> When they went, I heard the noise of their wings, like the noise of many waters, like the voice of the Almighty, a tumult like the noise of an army; and when they stood still, they let down their wings. (Ezekiel 1:24)

This shows the power and the greatness of these four creatures; their movement created an indescribable noise that Ezekiel could not find precise words to illustrate; he said, it is *like* the roar of rushing waters, more *like* the voice of the Almighty, perhaps *like* the tumult of an army.

> A voice came from above the firmament that was over their heads; whenever they stood, they let down their wings. (Ezekiel 1:25)

The voice above is coming from the throne of Almighty God. The wings they let down are not the ones forming the dome carrying the throne of God; they let down the wings stretched out to each other. When they are not in motion, these wings do not need to remain connected.

> And above the firmament over their heads was the likeness of a throne, in appearance like a

> sapphire stone; on the likeness of the throne
> was a likeness with the appearance of a man
> high above. (Ezekiel 1:26)

Here, Ezekiel describes the appearance of the throne like a sapphire stone, in the same manner Moses and the elders of Israel saw it (Exodus 24:10). The sapphire stone represents purity, magnificence, and beauty.

> Also from the appearance of His waist and
> upward I saw, as it were, the color of amber with
> the appearance of fire all around within it; and
> from the appearance of His waist and downward
> I saw, as it were, the appearance of fire with
> brightness all around. (Ezekiel 1:27)

Here, Ezekiel describes Him who is seated on the throne in appearance as that "of a man" (in knowledge and intellect) in "the color of amber" (in justice, stability, and fairness) with "fire all around" (in the destructive power of fire).

> Like the appearance of a rainbow in a cloud
> on a rainy day, so was the appearance of the
> brightness all around it. This was the appearance
> of the likeness of the glory of the Lord. So when
> I saw it, I fell on my face, and I heard a voice of
> One speaking. (Ezekiel 1:28)

The "appearance of a rainbow in a cloud" is symbolic of God's mercies. Today, LGBTQ+ supporters also use the sign of the rainbow, yet notice that their original rainbow was six colors while God's rainbow is seven colors. Satan is trying to imitate God in everything in order to deceive the people so that when they see the rainbow they will remember LGBTQ+ instead of remembering the mercies of God. Satan is a deceiver, and he likes to deceive us. God blinded their minds to make it six colors; the missing color was the color of heaven—blue. If they do not repent, they have no portion in heaven.

This is a vision God revealed to Ezekiel. From here, we take some of the church hymns, such as "He who sits upon the Cherubim." When John, in the *Revelation*, saw the throne, he did not see it the same way—He saw four creatures, each one with a unique face, and they were still carrying the throne of God. Isaiah saw the Seraph at the altar (but here there was no altar) who took a hot coal and touched the lips of Isaiah the prophet. Moses saw God as amber and sapphire stone. What we would like to say is that all the visions are more or less the same, but God showed different variations to different prophets, depending on the message He meant for each one.

There is no altar in heaven for communion because there is no need for forgiveness in heaven, yet there are various other altars—for judgment, for mercy, for prayer. "Given for us, for salvation, for remission of sins, and eternal life"; if we have made it to heaven, in eternal life, there is no longer a need for forgiveness.

The vision continues in the second and third chapters where God speaks to Ezekiel from upon the throne.

> But you, son of man, hear what I say to you. Do not be rebellious like that rebellious house; open your mouth and eat what I give you. Now when I looked, there was a hand stretched out to me; and behold, a scroll of a book was in it. Then He spread it before me; and there was writing on the inside and on the outside, and

written on it were lamentations and mourning and woe. (Ezekiel 2:8–10)

The *rebellious house* are the Israelites. He has a scroll in his hand, on which are written the hard times befalling the people of Israel due to their sins.

Moreover He said to me, "Son of man, eat what you find; eat this scroll, and go, speak to the house of Israel." So I opened my mouth, and He caused me to eat that scroll. (Ezekiel 3:1–2)

Ezekiel eats the scroll as instructed.

And He said to me, "Son of man, feed your belly, and fill your stomach with this scroll that I give you." So I ate, and it was in my mouth like honey in sweetness. (Ezekiel 3:3)

Imagine this scroll full of lamentations, mourning, and woe, but eating it, Ezekiel found it very sweet as honey. Why? Because he anticipated that the people of Israel, learning of the lamentations, mourning, and woe coming upon them, would offer repentance. Ezekiel thanked God and rejoiced that He was revealing this to the people; this joy made the scroll taste sweet. Unfortunately, the people did not benefit from God's declaration and warning.

Then the Spirit lifted me up, and I heard behind me a great thunderous voice: "Blessed is the glory of the Lord from His place!" (Ezekiel 3:12)

This was after he finished his conversation with God. During the Psalmody, we similarly say, "Blessed is the holy Name of Your glory" (in the third Canticle).

> I also heard the noise of the wings of the living creatures that touched one another, and the noise of the wheels beside them, and a great thunderous noise. So the Spirit lifted me up and took me away, and I went in bitterness, in the heat of my spirit; but the hand of the Lord was strong upon me. Then I came to the captives at Tel Abib, who dwelt by the River Chebar; and I sat where they sat, and remained there astonished among them seven days. (Ezekiel 3:13–15)

"The hand of the Lord was strong" means Ezekiel felt a strong presence of the Lord, such that he could not avoid or escape from this responsibility. Ezekiel was astonished; after he ate the scroll and found it sweet, God told him that the people of Israel were rebellious. Even though Ezekiel will reveal to them the contents of the scroll, they will not listen or repent. He spent seven days indecisive if he should inform them or not, since they will not listen anyway.

> Now it came to pass at the end of seven days that the word of the Lord came to me, saying, "Son of man, I have made you a watchman for the house of Israel; therefore hear a word from My mouth, and give them warning from Me: When I say to the wicked, 'You shall surely die,' and you give him no warning, nor speak to warn the wicked from his wicked way, to save his life, that same wicked man shall die in his iniquity; but his blood I will require at your hand. Yet, if you warn the wicked, and he does not turn from

his wickedness, nor from his wicked way, he shall die in his iniquity; but you have delivered your soul." (Ezekiel 3:16–19)

These words are beneficial to the clergy and servants. If God says to the wicked person, "You shall surely die," and you do not warn him, the wicked person will die in his wickedness, but you will be responsible for his blood, because you did not warn him. If you do warn him and he continues in his wickedness and does not listen, then you will have saved yourself.

> Again, when a righteous man turns from his righteousness and commits iniquity, and I lay a stumbling block before him, he shall die; because you did not give him warning, he shall die in his sin, and his righteousness which he has done shall not be remembered; but his blood I will require at your hand. Nevertheless if you warn the righteous man that the righteous should not sin, and he does not sin, he shall surely live because he took warning; also you will have delivered your soul. (Ezekiel 3:20–21)

The same applies for the righteous person.

> Then the hand of the Lord was upon me there, and He said to me, "Arise, go out into the plain, and there I shall talk with you." So I arose and went out into the plain, and behold, the glory of the Lord stood there, like the glory which I saw by the River Chebar; and I fell on my face. Then the Spirit entered me and set me on my feet, and spoke with me and said to me: "Go, shut yourself inside your house." (Ezekiel 3:22–24)

When he warns them, they will bind him with ropes because they do not want to hear his words or listen to him. If they will bind him, God will also bind his mouth, not to speak, because they do not deserve to hear.

> And you, O son of man, surely they will put ropes on you and bind you with them, so that you cannot go out among them. I will make your tongue cling to the roof of your mouth, so that you shall be mute and not be one to rebuke them, for they are a rebellious house. (Ezekiel 3:25–26)

God does not force people to listen to Him; if they do not listen, they are the ones who suffer loss. Neither will they receive rebuke from Ezekiel.

> But when I speak with you, I will open your mouth, and you shall say to them, "Thus says the Lord God. 'He who hears, let him hear; and he who refuses, let him refuse; for they are a rebellious house.'" (Ezekiel 3:27)

When I allow you to speak, then speak to the rebellious people.

Chapter 4

Second Vision

And it came to pass in the sixth year, in the sixth month, on the fifth day of the month, as I sat in my house with the elders of Judah sitting before me, that the hand of the Lord God fell upon me there. Then I looked, and there was a likeness, like the appearance of fire—from the appearance of His waist and downward, fire; and from His waist and upward, like the appearance of brightness, like the color of amber. (Ezekiel 8:1–2)

When he says, "I looked," it means a new vision has begun.

He stretched out the form of a hand, and took me by a lock of my hair; and the Spirit lifted me up between earth and heaven, and brought me in visions of God to Jerusalem, to the door of the north gate of the inner court, where the seat of the image of jealousy was, which provokes to jealousy. (Ezekiel 8:3)

He was in Babylon, and the Lord brought him to Jerusalem, to the statue that provoked jealousy from the Lord because of it being worshipped. How can they bow down and worship a statue in Jerusalem; God is a jealous God!

> And behold, the glory of the God of Israel was there, like the vision that I saw in the plain. (Ezekiel 8:4)

We elaborated on this when discussing the first chapter of Ezekiel above.

> Then He said to me, "Son of man, lift your eyes now toward the north." So I lifted my eyes toward the north, and there, north of the altar gate, was this image of jealousy in the entrance. (Ezekiel 8:5)

This means the statue of jealousy was on the north side of the altar of burnt offering.

> Furthermore He said to me, "Son of man, do you see what they are doing, the great abominations that the house of Israel commits here, to make Me go far away from My sanctuary? Now turn again, you will see greater abominations." (Ezekiel 8:6)

Angry, the Lord asked Ezekiel, "Do you see what they are doing?" They think to worship another god next to my altar! But you will see things that are even more detestable. Is there another god to worship? How can I remain in the presence of another supposed god (the idol) that they worship in Jerusalem?

"For all the gods of the Gentiles are devils."[1] In another vision, Ezekiel saw the glory of the Lord depart from the temple, like a cloud moving gradually up until He completely departed from the altar; this, also found in the book of Ezekiel, is before the destruction of Jerusalem.

> So He brought me to the door of the court; and when I looked, there was a hole in the wall. Then He said to me, "Son of man, dig into the wall"; and when I dug into the wall, there was a door. And He said to me, "Go in, and see the wicked abominations which they are doing there." So I went in and saw, and there—every sort of creeping thing, abominable beasts, and all the idols of the house of Israel, portrayed all around on the walls. (Ezekiel 8:7–10)

Once Ezekiel found the hole in the wall, the Lord asked him to dig into it, and he found a door. He opened the door, entered, and saw all the images of the idols portrayed on the walls of the altar.

> And there stood before them seventy men of the elders of the house of Israel, and in their midst stood Jaazaniah the son of Shaphan. Each man had a censer in his hand, and a thick cloud of incense went up. (Ezekiel 8:11)

They are raising incense to the idols!

> Then He said to me, "Son of man, have you seen what the elders of the house of Israel do in

---

1   The Douay-Rheims 1899 American Edition (DRA) used for compatibility with the original Coptic.

> the dark, every man in the room of his idols? For
> they say, 'The Lord does not see us, the Lord has
> forsaken the land.'" (Ezekiel 8:12)

The elders of Israel thought when they hid in this inner room, God would not see them worshiping the idols. The foolishness of the people of Israel reached the point of them starting to worship idols, and the elders of Israel were the ones who raised the incense to these idols. After all God had done for them from the time they left Egypt, when He led them through the wilderness of Sinai and into the Promised Land, they still returned to worshiping idols. They were still captives to this vice.

> And He said to me, "Turn again, and you will
> see greater abominations that they are doing."
> So He brought me to the door of the north gate
> of the Lord's house; and to my dismay, women
> were sitting there weeping for Tammuz. (Ezekiel
> 8:13–14)

This is all within the sanctuary! Tammuz is Babylon's god of fertility. There is an ancient legend that says Tammuz was in conflict with the god of death (Mot). If Tammuz is present, then Mot is not present; this being the mystery behind the changing seasons. During the conflict, Mot was able to kill and bury Tammuz, causing the trees to wither and die. The goddess of love, Ishtar, loved Tammuz, so she went into the underworld and revived Tammuz from death, reviving the trees (since he is the god of fertility). The hotter the weather and the more the leaves withered (Mot killing Tammuz), the more the women mourned Tammuz's *death* and sought his resurrection.

When the hot season ends, the priests of Tammuz come at night, open the tomb of Tammuz, and claim that Tammuz rose from the dead; greenery thrives as a sign of his resurrection. They go around touching the lips of people with the balsam saying, "Just as Tammuz rose, you also will rise from the dead, and vegetation and plenty will return to the ground." People rejoiced, and women rejoiced to the point that some women vowed themselves to Tammuz; since Tammuz is the god of fertility, part of Tammuz's worship was excessive debauchery. They were mourning for Tammuz, awaiting him to restore fertility and agriculture; although Tammuz cannot see or have any power to do anything, he is a god of fertility! Instead of praising God for fertility, the Israelite women imitated the Gentile women in praising Tammuz!

> Then He said to me, "Have you seen this, O son of man? Turn again, you will see greater abominations than these." So He brought me into the inner court of the Lord's house; and there, at the door of the temple of the Lord, between the porch and the altar, were about twenty-five men with their backs toward the temple of the Lord and their faces toward the east, and they were worshiping the sun toward the east. (Ezekiel 8:15–16)

The entrance to the temple was from the east; in the Old Testament, the Israelites worshiped towards the west, giving their backs to the Garden of Eden—from which Adam and Eve were evicted. After reconciliation, Adam was restored to paradise, so we worship toward the east. Those twenty-five men gave their backs to the temple of the Lord facing east and worshiped the sun.

And He said to me, "Have you seen this, O son of man? Is it a trivial thing to the house of Judah to commit the abominations which they commit here? For they have filled the land with violence; then they have returned to provoke Me to anger. Indeed they put the branch to their nose." (Ezekiel 8:17)

What does putting "the branch to their nose" mean? Sun worshippers claimed that life comes from the sun god, and at night, when the sun sets, life continues in the branches of the trees. Life comes from the branch that receives life and chlorophyll from the sun; they bring the branch to their nose to indicate life continuing even if they cannot see the sun. These are all idolatrous traditions, and the Israelites anger God by practicing these traditions. Instead of worshiping God as the source of life, they worship the sun.

Therefore I also will act in fury. My eye will not spare nor will I have pity; and though they cry in My ears with a loud voice, I will not hear them. (Ezekiel 8:18)

The people offered incense to the idols, worshiped the statue of jealousy, mourned the god Tammuz, worshiped the sun, and brought the branch to their noses, so the Lord told Ezekiel that He was angry at Israel and would punish them.

Then He called out in my hearing with a loud voice, saying, "Let those who have charge over the city draw near, each with a deadly weapon in his hand." (Ezekiel 9:1)

Calling out in a loud voice indicates the importance of the upcoming words of the vision.

> And suddenly six men came from the direction of the upper gate, which faces north, each with his battle-ax in his hand. One man among them was clothed with linen and had a writer's inkhorn at his side. They went in and stood beside the bronze altar. Now the glory of the God of Israel had gone up from the cherub, where it had been, to the threshold of the temple. And He called to the man clothed with linen, who had the writer's inkhorn at his side. (Ezekiel 9:2–3)

Who are the six men? They are angels. As there is a guardian angel to protect each human being, there are guardian angels appointed by God to guard the city; the six angels are the ones appointed as guardians over Jerusalem. He called those, with their deadly weapons in their hands, because God had decided to destroy the people. "The glory of the God of Israel had gone up from the cherub" is the Lord initiating His departure from the temple.

> And the Lord said to him, "Go through the midst of the city, through the midst of Jerusalem, and put a mark on the foreheads of the men who sigh and cry over all the abominations that are done within it." To the others He said in my hearing, "Go after him through the city and kill; do not let your eye spare, nor have any pity." (Ezekiel 9:4–5)

He sent out the one in linen to go throughout Jerusalem and put a mark on the foreheads of those who grieve and lament over all the abominations done by those who worship the idols. Next, He ordered the six angels who have the deadly weapons to kill (without showing pity or compassion) anyone who does not have that mark.

> "Utterly slay old and young men, maidens and little children and women; but do not come near anyone on whom is the mark; and begin at My sanctuary." So they began with the elders who were before the temple. (Ezekiel 9:6)

The commandment is to slaughter all, but not to touch anyone who has the mark (the sign of the Holy Spirit). Begin at My sanctuary; begin with those who are desecrating the temple.

> Then He said to them, "Defile the temple, and fill the courts with the slain. Go out!" And they went out and killed in the city. So it was, that while they were killing them, I was left alone; and I fell on my face and cried out, and said, "Ah, Lord God! Will You destroy all the remnant of Israel in pouring out Your fury on Jerusalem?" (Ezekiel 9:7–8)

Here Ezekiel intercedes to the Lord.

> Then He said to me, "The iniquity of the house of Israel and Judah is exceedingly great, and the land is full of bloodshed, and the city full of perversity; for they say, 'The Lord has forsaken the land, and the Lord does not see!' And as for Me also, My eye will neither spare, nor will I have pity, but I will recompense their deeds on their own head." Just then, the man clothed with

> linen, who had the inkhorn at his side, reported back and said, "I have done as You commanded me." (Ezekiel 9:9–11)

This man in linen, also an angel, answered God, indicating that he had done all he had been ordered.

Keep in mind that in John the Theologian's *Revelation*, the door to the tabernacle opened and seven angels went out dressed in linen. A scroll had the names of those who were marked on the forehead so that no harm would come to them, as we read, "Of the tribe of Judah twelve thousand were sealed... of the tribe... twelve thousand were sealed" (Revelation 7:5–8). We understand that angels do participate in wars, famines, and pandemics, according to God's providence, to lead people to repentance.

Ezekiel interceded before God, but since the evil of Israel was great, God said, "My eye will not spare nor will I have pity" (Ezekiel 8:18). People dying while Ezekiel was standing there reminds us of Psalm 91:7: "A thousand may fall at your side, and ten thousand at your right hand; but it shall not come near you."

> And I looked, and there in the firmament that was above the head of the cherubim, there appeared something like a sapphire stone, having the appearance of the likeness of a throne. Then He spoke to the man clothed with linen, and said, "Go in among the wheels, under the cherub, fill your hands with coals of fire from among the cherubim, and scatter them over the city." And he went in as I watched. (Ezekiel 10:1–2)

God asked the angel to fill his hands with burning coals from among the cherubim and scatter them over the city—this indicates God's divine wrath. We know that the cherubim are immersed in fire. The man in linen entered before Ezekiel's eyes.

> Now the cherubim were standing on the south side of the temple when the man went in, and the cloud filled the inner court. Then the glory of the Lord went up from the cherub, and paused over the threshold of the temple; and the house was filled with the cloud, and the court was full of the brightness of the Lord's glory. And the sound of the wings of the cherubim was heard even in the outer court, like the voice of Almighty God when He speaks. Then it happened, when He commanded the man clothed in linen, saying, "Take fire from among the wheels, from among the cherubim," that he went in and stood beside the wheels. And the cherub stretched out his hand from among the cherubim to the fire that was among the cherubim, and took some of it and put it into the hands of the man clothed with linen, who took it and went out. The cherubim appeared to have the form of a man's hand under their wings. (Ezekiel 10:3–8)

The cherub stretched out the hand under his wing; this is how Ezekiel realized that there is a hand under the wing.

> And when I looked, there were four wheels by the cherubim, one wheel by one cherub and another wheel by each other cherub; the wheels appeared to have the color of a beryl stone. As for their appearance, all four looked alike—as it

> were, a wheel in the middle of a wheel. (Ezekiel 10:9–10)

We explained this before.

> When they went, they went toward any of their four directions; they did not turn aside when they went, but followed in the direction the head was facing. They did not turn aside when they went. And their whole body, with their back, their hands, their wings, and the wheels that the four had, were full of eyes all around. (Ezekiel 10:11–12)

The eyes are symbolic of knowledge; the cherubim are full of knowledge.

> As for the wheels, they were called in my hearing, "Wheel." Each one had four faces: the first face was the face of a cherub, the second face the face of a man, the third the face of a lion, and the fourth the face of an eagle. And the cherubim were lifted up. This was the living creature I saw by the River Chebar. When the cherubim went, the wheels went beside them; and when the cherubim lifted their wings to mount up from the earth, the same wheels also did not turn from beside them. When the cherubim stood still, the wheels stood still, and when one was lifted up, the other lifted itself up, for the spirit of the living creature was in them. Then the glory of the Lord departed from the threshold of the temple and stood over the cherubim. (Ezekiel 10:13–18)

It is very saddening to watch God leave the temple gradually because of the evil occurring within.

> And the cherubim lifted their wings and mounted up from the earth in my sight. When they went out, the wheels were beside them; and they stood at the door of the east gate of the Lord's house, and the glory of the God of Israel was above them. This is the living creature I saw under the God of Israel by the River Chebar, and I knew they were cherubim. Each one had four faces and each one four wings, and the likeness of the hands of a man was under their wings. And the likeness of their faces was the same as the faces which I had seen by the River Chebar, their appearance and their persons. They each went straight forward. (Ezekiel 10:19–22)

The vision continues in the next chapter.

> Then the Spirit lifted me up and brought me to the East Gate of the Lord's house, which faces eastward; and there at the door of the gate were twenty-five men, among whom I saw Jaazaniah the son of Azzur, and Pelatiah the son of Benaiah, princes of the people. And He said to me: "Son of man, these are the men who devise iniquity and give wicked counsel in this city." (Ezekiel 11:1–2)

Jaazaniah, the son of Azzur, was previously mentioned offering incense to the idols. These people were giving wicked advice to the city, so God asked Ezekiel to prophesy against them.

> "Who say, 'The time is not near to build houses; this city is the caldron, and we are the meat.' Therefore prophesy against them, prophesy, O son of man!" Then the Spirit of the Lord fell upon me, and said to me, "Speak! 'Thus says the Lord: "Thus you have said, O house of Israel; for I know the things that come into your mind."'"
> (Ezekiel 11:3–5)

I am aware of all your thoughts!

> "You have multiplied your slain in this city, and you have filled its streets with the slain." Therefore thus says the Lord God: "Your slain whom you have laid in its midst, they are the meat, and this city is the caldron; but I shall bring you out of the midst of it." (Ezekiel 11:6–7)

I will drive you out of Jerusalem! What is meant by the meat and the caldron? When they say, "The time is not near to build houses," they are ridiculing the prophecy of Jeremiah and Ezekiel that said the city would be destroyed! They are claiming the city will not be destroyed, and so, they refuse to rebuild their houses. In ridiculing the words of Jeremiah and Ezekiel, they are disregarding the words of God.

Next they said, "This city is the caldron, and we are the meat." Jeremiah prophesied that Jerusalem is the pot that will be destroyed: "'What do you see?' And I said, 'I see a boiling pot, and it is facing away from the north'" (Jeremiah 1:13). The people mocked Jeremiah, saying, "If Jerusalem is the caldron, and we are the meat inside the boiling caldron, then we are protected since no one would dare extend his hand and pull out the meat (that is us) from the pot!" This is why they figured neither the Pharaoh nor Nebuchadnezzar would be able to extend his hand to Jerusalem and evict them. God retorted their mockery: "You have multiplied your slain in this city… they are the meat, and this city is the caldron." The meat are the dead bodies of those whom you have slain as human sacrifices to the idols in Jerusalem, in the caldron—God said I will take you out of Jerusalem to be exiled to Babylon.

> This city shall not be your caldron, nor shall you be the meat in its midst. I will judge you at the border of Israel. (Ezekiel 11:11)

Jerusalem will not be the caldron, and you will not be the meat.

> And you shall know that I am the Lord; for you have not walked in My statutes nor executed My judgments, but have done according to the customs of the Gentiles which are all around you. (Ezekiel 11:12)

Chapter 5

Fourth Vision: The Eastern Gate

Earlier we covered Ezekiel's third vision concerning the dried bones (in the bird's-eye view of his signs), so we come to the fourth vision. Most people are familiar with it; about St. Mary's perpetual virginity, it is mentioned in Ezekiel 40.

After the destruction of Jerusalem, the Lord's hand being against this city, God wanted to give hope to Ezekiel. He took him to the top of a very high mountain where he saw a man who seemed to be made of bronze, whose hand held a linen thread and a measuring reed. God showed him the building of the house of the Lord, including its encompassing fence, the doors, the eastern gate, the rooms, and all the details found in chapters 40, 41, and 42 of Ezekiel.

> Afterward he brought me to the gate, the gate that faces toward the east. And behold, the glory of the God of Israel came from the way of the east. His voice was like the sound of many waters; and the earth shone with His glory. It was like the appearance of the vision which I

saw—like the vision which I saw when I came to destroy the city. The visions were like the vision which I saw by the River Chebar; and I fell on my face. And the glory of the Lord came into the temple by way of the gate which faces toward the east. The Spirit lifted me up and brought me into the inner court; and behold, the glory of the Lord filled the temple. Then I heard Him speaking to me from the temple, while a man stood beside me. And He said to me, "Son of man, this is the place of My throne and the place of the soles of My feet, where I will dwell in the midst of the children of Israel forever. No more shall the house of Israel defile My holy name, they nor their kings, by their harlotry or with the carcasses of their kings on their high places. When they set their threshold by My threshold, and their doorpost by My doorpost, with a wall between them and Me, they defiled My holy name by the abominations which they committed; therefore I have consumed them in My anger. Now let them put their harlotry and the carcasses of their kings far away from Me, and I will dwell in their midst forever." (Ezekiel 43:1–9)

The Lord here explained why He destroyed the old house of Israel forever.

Then He brought me back to the outer gate of the sanctuary which faces toward the east, but it was shut. And the Lord said to me, "This gate shall be shut; it shall not be opened, and no man

> shall enter by it, because the Lord God of Israel
> has entered by it; therefore it shall be shut."
> (Ezekiel 44:1-2)

All church fathers elaborate on the meaning of the eastern door, saying it represents the virginity of St. Mary; Christ entered her, lived inside her, and left her without affecting her virginity. St. Mary was a virgin before, during, and after giving birth to Christ. St. Mary's icon has three stars, representing her virginity before, during, and after birth. Occasionally, two stars are drawn, and the third star is the Lord Christ. One might find either icon.

Concerning the structure of our churches, in constructing a new church, it should not have doors on the east side. The church should have three doors: west, north, and south; there should be no door in the east.

This vision concerning the temple was in the twenty-fifth year of exile. Nebuchadnezzar, the king of Babylon, had taken captive Jehoiachin, along with many people, seized the expensive utensils of the house of the Lord, and made Zedekiah king (2 Chronicles 36:10–11). Thereafter, Zedekiah rebelled against Nebuchadnezzar, so Nebuchadnezzar went up to Jerusalem, killed its inhabitants, burned the house of the Lord and the palaces, destroyed the wall around Jerusalem, destroyed all the valuable utensils, and took all the people to exile.

The captivity occurred in two stages: one during the reign of Jehoiachin and one during the reign of Zedekiah. Nebuchadnezzar did not destroy the city or burn the temple the first time, but did so eleven years later during the second captivity. Thereafter, the hand of God came upon Ezekiel, taking him to the land of Israel on a high mountain, so the vision would be clear to him. He saw an angel, bronze in appearance, in the form of a man with linen thread and a measuring reed. He showed him what would happen in Jerusalem when the temple is rebuilt; this would happen 45 years later. God showed Ezekiel that Zerubbabel would rebuild the temple after 45 years.

> And it was made with cherubim and palm trees, a palm tree between cherub and cherub. Each cherub had two faces, so that the face of a man was toward a palm tree on one side, and the face of a young lion toward a palm tree on the other side; thus it was made throughout the temple all around. (Ezekiel 41:18–19)

There were carvings of palm trees in the temple. As the Psalm says, "The righteous shall flourish like a palm tree, he shall grow like a cedar in Lebanon" (Psalm 92:12). The palm trees represent the righteous faithful ones who fear God and worship Him with pure clean hearts. Next to the palm trees were cherubim, for it says in the Psalm, "The angel of the Lord encamps all around those who fear Him, and delivers them" (Psalm 34:7). The palm trees represent the faithful while the cherub represents the angel of the Lord who encamps all around those who fear Him and delivers them.

We notice here that the cherub has two faces (man and lion), not four faces as in other chapters. The face of a man (human) represents knowledge, learning, and wisdom, while the lion represents strength; God deals with his people in wisdom and power. The man also represents guidance, while the lion represents protection, as in the Psalm: "Your rod and Your staff, they comfort me" (Psalm 23:4). The rod directs, and the staff supports.

> And behold, the glory of the God of Israel came from the way of the east. His voice was like the sound of many waters; and the earth shone with His glory. (Ezekiel 43:2)

All the appearances in the Old Testament belong to the hypostasis of the Son. The hypostasis of the Son is the Sun of Righteousness; He came from the east, as the sun sends its rays from the east.

> This gate shall be shut; it shall not be opened, and no man shall enter by it, because the Lord God of Israel has entered by it; therefore it shall be shut. As for the prince, because he is the prince, he may sit in it to eat bread before the Lord; he shall enter by way of the vestibule of the gateway, and go out the same way. (Ezekiel 44:2–3)

This shows the perpetual virginity of St. Mary as she gave birth to the Lord of Glory while her virginity was sealed. The prince is Christ who entered while the gate was shut. His sitting to eat bread speaks of the incarnation where He resembled us in everything. The vestibule is symbolic of the Jewish nation, because He will be incarnate from the Jewish people (from St. Mary) and live among them. He will "go out the same way," because the Jews are also the ones who crucified Him outside Jerusalem.

> Now say to the rebellious, to the house of Israel, "Thus says the Lord God: 'O house of Israel, let Us have no more of all your abominations. When you brought in foreigners, uncircumcised in heart and uncircumcised in flesh, to be in My

> sanctuary to defile it—My house—and when
> you offered My food, the fat and the blood, then
> they broke My covenant because of all your
> abominations.'" (Ezekiel 44:6-7)

Notice he said "uncircumcised in heart" before "uncircumcised in flesh" because the physical circumcision is only a symbol. In the New Testament, circumcision is symbolic of baptism, as St. Paul said, "In Him you were also circumcised with the circumcision made without hands, by putting off the body of the sins of the flesh, by the circumcision of Christ, buried with Him in baptism, in which you also were raised with Him through faith in the working of God, who raised Him from the dead" (Colossians 2:11-12). No one can be consecrated to serve God if not baptized. One uncircumcised in heart is one who does not believe in Christ; as such, he cannot serve.

Holy and Common:

We also need to dwell on a verse here because of its importance; one finds it in the same vision related to the perpetual virginity of St. Mary.

> It had a wall all around, five hundred cubits long
> and five hundred wide, to separate the holy
> areas from the common. (Ezekiel 42:20)

This is a very important expression; it is repeated multiple times in the Holy Bible. It is also mentioned in Leviticus: "That you may distinguish between holy and unholy, and between unclean and clean" (Leviticus 10:10).

In Ezekiel we read: "Her priests have violated My law and profaned My holy things; they have not distinguished between the holy and unholy" (Ezekiel 22:26).

It was also repeated in Ezekiel 43. Distinguishing between the holy and the common is a very important topic in God's mind. What is meant by these two terms? *Common* means something allowed while *holy* refers to something consecrated for God only. Not every common thing is holy, but every holy thing is common. For example, is it common to have a cup of tea? Yes. But could we take the communion chalice and use it for drinking tea? Not at all, because the chalice is holy. Could we sit at a desk and write letters? Yes. But could we use the altar as a desk? No, because it is holy. The Lord God wants us to distinguish between the Holy and the common.

Three factors distinguish the Holy and the common:
1 - Time
2 - Location
3 - Persons

1) Times and Days:

The day of the Lord is holy. Any sin committed on the day of the Lord is a two-fold sin. Why? Suppose one lied on Sunday. First, one sinned by telling a lie, and second, by not keeping the day of the Lord holy, as the Holy Bible says, "Remember the Sabbath day [day of the Lord], to keep it holy" (Exodus 20:8). We should be very careful concerning any sin committed during holy days, such as Sundays, fasting days, Passion Week, and feast days. This does not mean we can commit sins on the other days; rather, on these holy days, we should be more cautious and be more spiritually diligent.

During visitations, some people tell us they attend church on Wednesdays instead of Sundays because of crowdedness on Sundays. We tell them to continue going to church on Wednesdays, but they also need to go on Sunday, the Lord's Day. It is not acceptable to be home on Sunday while the church is celebrating the Divine Liturgy.

In Egypt, Friday is the official weekend, and all churches celebrate the Divine Liturgy on Friday, yet because our ancestors understood the importance of sanctifying Sunday, they insisted on celebrating the Divine Liturgy on Sunday, the Lord's Day. Because of their insistence, the government allowed them to arrive to work late (10 AM), to allow them to attend the Divine Liturgy on Sunday. This shows how our ancestors correctly understood the concept of the Lord's Day.

Sometimes, we notice people not attending the eve of feasts. A sick person's inability to attend is understandable, but laziness is not acceptable for not attending. It is also unacceptable to miss the events of Passion Week, such as the liturgies on Covenant Thursday and Bright Saturday. These are holy days. If we do not pray on these days, when will we pray? The Lord is not pleased with people's lack of understanding of the difference between the common and the holy.

2) Location:

Churches, in general, are places where we cannot place a table in the middle of the church and eat a meal; that is not acceptable because the church is a holy place. Monasteries are also our holy places. Listening to a sermon by His Holiness Pope Shenouda III, he narrated how a bus reached the monastery. Upon arrival, the servants asked the youngsters on the trip to go play ball. His Holiness asked the servant about those boys playing ball in the monastery and commented that the monastery is a holy place. The servant replied to His Holiness by asking if it were not written in the Holy Bible to "let the little children come to Me, and do not forbid them" (Matthew 19:14). The Pope answered, "Was it playing ball that He was saying not to forbid them from!" Again, what is acceptable in a common place is not fitting in a holy place.

Take for example, the general behavior or the dress code for those coming to the churches and monasteries for retreat. In these holy places, one walks gently, talks softly, and does not converse inside the church. In the church canons, those who smile (not so much as laugh) while serving in the altar are prohibited from serving for a week; meanwhile, we find people walking around the church, talking loudly, telling jokes, sleeping on the pews, etc. Where is the respect for God's house? The Psalm says, "Holiness adorns Your house, O Lord" (Psalm 93:5).

3) Persons:

There are individuals consecrated for God, like the Nazarites in the Old Testament; there was a law for the Nazarites. Sunday school servants should be distinguished from the rest of the congregation because they consecrated themselves to serve God. The bishop, priest, monastic, and the consecrated sisters and brothers are dedicated to serve God. The higher the rank, the greater one should observe holiness.

There are behaviors that are acceptable (common) by the non-clergy but are not acceptable for the clergy or consecrates. Sometimes, when we try to direct the attention of a Sunday school servant or of a monastic to a certain behavior that would be acceptable for the non-clergy, they question what is wrong with it. It is unacceptable for them because they chose to be consecrated to God, and the actions they are doing (which are not acceptable) are not holy. Therefore, they cannot carry out such actions. Just as we said before, it is acceptable to drink Coke, but not to drink Coke from the chalice; likewise, those who consecrate themselves for God should watch their behavior because what is acceptable to others may not be acceptable for them; it does not befit their consecration.

This is concerning the verse about the common and the holy. Next, God indicated the requirements for the priests to Ezekiel.

> "But the priests, the Levites, the sons of Zadok, who kept charge of My sanctuary when the children of Israel went astray from Me, they shall come near Me to minister to Me; and they shall stand before Me to offer to Me the fat and the blood," says the Lord God. "They shall enter My sanctuary, and they shall come near My table to minister to Me, and they shall keep My charge." (Ezekiel 44:15-16)

Only those who remain faithful servants, while all others stray, are permitted to serve the Lord.

> And it shall be, whenever they enter the gates of the inner court, that they shall put on linen garments; no wool shall come upon them while they minister within the gates of the inner court

or within the house. (Ezekiel 44:17)

Linen is white, indicative of purity, "Blessed are the pure in heart" (Matthew 5:8), as we read that the 24 elders seated on the thrones in heaven were "clothed in white robes" (Revelation 4:4). Even today, we still wear white when we enter the sanctuary.

> They shall have linen turbans on their heads and linen trousers on their bodies; they shall not clothe themselves with anything that causes sweat. (Ezekiel 44:18)

These are all for chastity. The linen turbans on their heads are the crown of the priesthood. Linen trousers are to cover the priest when ascending the steps of the altar and bending over the altar. They also should not wear anything that makes them sweat; sweat is not comfortable, and clingy, sweaty, wet clothes are not appropriate.

> When they go out to the outer court, to the outer court to the people, they shall take off their garments in which they have ministered, leave them in the holy chambers, and put on other garments; and in their holy garments they shall not sanctify the people. (Ezekiel 44:19)

Priests and clergy remove their white garments once the service is completed, and don the black garments. The priest should not go around blessing people or exit the church while still wearing the white (service) clothes.

> They shall neither shave their heads nor let their hair grow long, but they shall keep their hair well trimmed. (Ezekiel 44:20)

This is the law of the Nazarite in the Old Testament. They grow their hair, but should not try to style it. There are clergy who do not groom or trim their beard from the day of their consecration; this is the correct authentic way.

> No priest shall drink wine when he enters the inner court. (Ezekiel 44:21)

He does not drink wine to avoid drunkenness since he should act with exactness and be a role model for the people.

> They shall not take as wife a widow or a divorced woman, but take virgins of the descendants of the house of Israel, or widows of priests. And they shall teach My people the difference between the holy and the unholy, and cause them to discern between the unclean and the clean. (Ezekiel 44:22-23)

It is the priest's and the servants' responsibility to teach the congregation the difference between the holy and the common. Sadly, it is rare that someone teaches the difference, although God says this is our responsibility.

> In controversy they shall stand as judges, and judge it according to My judgments. They shall keep My laws and My statutes in all My appointed meetings, and they shall hallow My Sabbaths. (Ezekiel 44:24)

They should judge according to God's judgment, not according to their own viewpoint.

They shall not defile themselves by coming near a dead person. Only for father or mother, for son or daughter, for brother or unmarried sister may they defile themselves. (Ezekiel 44:25)

This is part of the Nazarite vow: (1) drink no wine, (2) not shave the hair of his head, and (3) not touch a dead body.

"After he is cleansed, they shall count seven days for him. And on the day that he goes to the sanctuary to minister in the sanctuary, he must offer his sin offering in the inner court," says the Lord God. "It shall be, in regard to their inheritance, that I am their inheritance. You shall give them no possession in Israel, for I am their possession." (Ezekiel 44:26-28)

Verse 28 applies particularly to monastics; the Lord God is their possession, their inheritance. Monastics should not have possessions, no bank account, no title deeds; they come completely relying on the Lord. The Lord also provides for the clergy, as "the Lord has commanded that those who preach the gospel should live from the gospel... Who plants a vineyard and does not eat of its fruit? Or who tends a flock and does not drink of the milk of the flock? ...If we have sown spiritual things for you, is it a great thing if we reap your material things?" (1 Corinthians 9:14, 7, 11). This is a beautiful promise, that "I Am their possession. I Am their inheritance, so they should not search for any other." Next, He assured them.

They shall eat the grain offering, the sin offering, and the trespass offering; every dedicated thing in Israel shall be theirs. (Ezekiel 44:29)

The Lord allotted certain items for the clergy that are not given to the general public.

> The best of all firstfruits of any kind, and every sacrifice of any kind from all your sacrifices, shall be the priest's; also you shall give to the priest the first of your ground meal, to cause a blessing to rest on your house. (Ezekiel 44:30)

Sometimes people see clergy wearing a certain fabric, for instance, and they murmur about the cost, but notice that here God said to "give to the priest the first... the best." St. Paul answered such people: "Not that I seek the gift, but I seek the fruit that abounds to your account... I have learned both to be full and to be hungry, both to abound and to suffer need." (Philippians 4:17, 12)

Others think we encourage almsgiving because we are in need; even if all the people refrained from giving, God will still take care of His people. God took care of Elijah and prevented the bin of flour and the jar of oil from running out throughout the drought. Sending out the disciples for the first time, the Lord commanded them to take neither silver nor gold; when they returned He asked them, "Did you lack anything?" (Luke 22:35). God will accomplish His will regardless of whether people donate or not. So then, why does the church ask for donations? It is for the people to receive a blessing, in addition to it being a commandment by God. We give to the priest, not because he is in need, but to receive blessing. In the early Church, during the famine, people did not travel to Jerusalem to give to the poor, but Paul and Barnabas received the collection and took it to Jerusalem, and in doing so, they indirectly gave it to the poor.

The priests shall not eat anything, bird or beast, that died naturally or was torn by wild beasts. (Ezekiel 44:31)

Chapter 6

Fifth Vision

We, however, forgot to mention that the meaning of the name Ezekiel is "God gives strength"; amid all weaknesses and being in captivity, Ezekiel was able to tolerate everything and remain faithful through God's strength while being away from the Lord's altar. One might ask why God kept calling Ezekiel "son of man." The answer is simple: it is to remind Ezekiel that he is weak and needs God, so God can strengthen him. In fact, to remind him of that, God called Ezekiel "son of man" more than 90 times in the book.

We spoke about four of Ezekiel's visions, and now we conclude the discussion of the book of Ezekiel with the fifth vision, which is in chapter 47.

> Then he brought me back to the door of the temple; and there was water, flowing from under the threshold of the temple toward the east, for the front of the temple faced east; the water was flowing from under the right side of the temple, south of the altar. (Ezekiel 47:1)

After the angel showed Ezekiel "the house," the temple, he then brought him back to the door of the temple, and there was water flowing from under the threshold of the temple toward the east. As we mentioned before, the temple was facing toward the west, so the door is toward the east, and the water running under the temple is on the east side, because the entrance of the house is on the east side, and the water is flowing from under the right side of the temple. What does this all mean? Let us consider it one bit at a time to understand it.

First, the angel returned Ezekiel to the entrance of the temple. Doors were built for the temple (Old Testament) and the church (New Testament); how else would people be able to enter—to represent acceptance of those who are returning to God—the penitent, the believers. The doors are always open, "and the one who comes to Me I will by no means cast out" (John 6:37). The church has three doors, resembling the Holy Trinity—one on the west side, one on the north side, and the third on the south side. Only three doors. There is no door on the east side—this resembles the virginity of St. Mary. We notice here that the angel is the one who brought Ezekiel back to the entrance of the house (church). This is the role of the priest, the servants, and the consecrated individuals—to bring people back to the door of the church (Christ) because Jesus said, "No one comes to the Father except through me"—He is the only way leading to eternal life.

After that, he finds that the water is flowing from under the threshold of the temple toward the east side of the temple. The water represents the blessings and grace—they come out of the church. Those blessings are coming from the presence of God because the church is the house of God. The water is at floor level, indicating that only the humble individual at ground level bowing down will receive such blessings; the arrogant will not receive any blessings.

The water is coming out from the right side of the house stemming from the right altar. The altar represents the cross on which Christ offered Himself as a sacrifice. All blessings come from our faith in the cross: "God forbid that I should boast except in the cross of our Lord Jesus Christ" (Galatians 6:14). It is the right side, because out of His right side flowed blood and water. The blood is for forgiveness of sins and the water is a sign of life. The water represents baptism, and the blood represents Communion. It is as if the prophet was seeing the pierced right side of Christ with its life-giving blood (the water represents life) overflowing from under the threshold of the house (the church), to benefit the humble.

> He brought me out by way of the north gate, and led me around on the outside to the outer gateway that faces east; and there was water, running out on the right side. And when the man went out to the east with the line in his hand, he measured one thousand cubits, and he brought me through the waters; the water came up to my ankles. Again he measured one thousand and brought me through the waters; the water came up to my knees. Again he measured one thousand and brought me through; the water came up to my waist. Again he measured one thousand, and it was a river that I could not cross; for the water was too deep, water in which one must swim, a river that could not be crossed. (Ezekiel 47:2–5)

There are four stages:

1 - First measurement: Water up to the ankle

2 - Second measurement—water up to the knee

3 - Third measurement—water up to the waist

4 - Water that cannot be crossed

What do these four stages mean? They represent the four stages of spiritual growth. Let us look at them one stage at a time.

First Stage (Repentance): Water up to the ankle

The ankle reminds us of the struggle between us (humans) and Satan, God told the serpent, "I will put enmity between you and the woman, and between your seed and her Seed; He shall bruise your head, and you shall bruise His *heel*" (Genesis 3:15). Water to the ankle is the first step toward spiritual growth; the individual is reminded of the fall of Adam and all humanity, but salvation is prepared where the offspring of Eve (Christ) will crush the head of Satan. Recall that when Peter lifted up and healed the lame man at the door of the Beautiful Gate, "immediately his feet and *ankle* bones received strength. So he, leaping up, stood and walked… walking, leaping, and praising God" (Acts 3:7-8). The ankle reminds us of God's work, reviving us from spiritual paralysis; God will give us strength as He gave to the lame person. So, the water that is up to the ankle (the work of grace) reminds us of the fall of humanity, salvation through Christ, spiritual struggle, rescue from spiritual paralysis, and being granted strength which in turn is conveyed in thanksgiving to God.

Second Stage (Communion, Prayer, and Fasting): Water up to the knee

What do the knees represent? In 2 Samuel 22:37, we read, "You enlarged my path under me; so my feet [knees] did not slip." The knees represent the steadfastness in the new life. Our Lord said, "If you abide in Me, and My words abide in you, you will ask what you desire, and it shall be done for you" (John 15:7). Abiding in Him comes through communion: "He who eats My flesh and drinks My blood abides in Me, and I in him" (John 6:56). The first meaning of the knee is abiding in Christ.

The second meaning of the knee is mentioned in Isaiah 45:23, "To Me every knee shall bow," therefore, the knees remind us of the importance of prayer in the life of the faithful. Daniel also "went home. And in his upper room… he knelt down on his knees three times that day, and prayed" (Daniel 6:10). The believer needs prayer in order to grow.

The third meaning of the knees reminds us of fasting and contrition before God, for Him to have mercy and compassion on us. The psalmist says, "My knees are weak through fasting" (Psalm 109:24). The knees mean prayers and fasting; fasting and prayer are the two wings by which a person could become more noble-minded than the earthly things. As our Master said, "This kind can come out only by prayers and fasting." The knees have three meanings: (a) communion, (b) prayer, and (c) fasting. This is the second stage, which means the person, through communion, prayer, and fasting is elevated in the spiritual life.

Third Stage (Readiness, Watchfulness, and Humbleness): Water up to the waist

The waist is a symbol of readiness. "Let your waist be girded and your lamps burning" (Luke 12:35). When God told the Israelites to depart from Egypt, He said, "And thus you shall eat it: with a belt on your waist, your sandals on your feet, and your staff in your hand" (Exodus 12:11). This is a symbol of perfect readiness to depart and of being watchful—"Watch therefore, for you know neither the day nor the hour in which the Son of Man is coming" (Matthew 25:13). It can also mean preparation for communion. St. Paul writes, "Stand therefore, having girded your waist with truth, having put on the breastplate of righteousness" (Ephesians 14:6); *truth* refers to Christ: "I am the way, the truth, and the life" (John 14:6)—the life of watchfulness and vigil cannot be reached except through Christ. St. John the Baptist, who was famous for his humbleness, also used to wear "a leather belt around his waist" (Matthew 3:4). Additionally, when they told Jacob, falsely, that Joseph was killed, he "tore his clothes, put sackcloth on his waist" (Genesis 7:34). The waist, in addition to representing watchfulness, can also symbolize compunction and humbleness.

Fourth Stage: Water that cannot be crossed

The excessive water which no one could cross refers to the overflow of grace. The person is covered completely with water, meaning the ego has died within the individual and everything related to the materialistic, earthly, and perishable is completely gone.

Where were we born? We were born in the baptismal font, in the water. As fish die if kept away from water, if we leave the grace of the water, of the Holy Spirit, we will die, because we were born at baptism. People can grow until they are completely immersed with water, and the ego dies.

For this reason, in the first three stages, the ego always says "me and not the others." At the beginning of our repentance, we search for our own. When some servants or monastics confess, they say, "*I* would never have imagined that *I* would commit such a sin!" They are not sorry for committing a sin against God, they are incredulous that *they* committed such a sin—they do not see the self as weak, and this is the problem with the ego. Again, if a person says something inappropriate to his father, he does not see himself as weak, but rather will be sad during the confession not because of the hurt caused to his father but rather because of the shock over having uttered such a comment; he is upset because it hurts *his* ego. For that reason, in the fraction prayer we say, "Be sorrowful, O my soul, for your sins that caused these sufferings to Your compassionate Redeemer"—not because your inflated ego fell into this sin.

The first stage (ankles) is "me, not the others." In the second stage (knees), the individual says, "It is me and then the others—I serve myself and I can also serve others." In the third stage (waist), "It is the others and then me." There is gradual humbling here because the waist represents humbleness—I put the others first, and I can sacrifice myself for them. In the fourth stage (overflow), one is grace-filled and so says, "It is no longer I who live, but Christ lives in me" (Galatians 2:20); the others are everything, and I am not important at all.

Let us look at St. Stephen at the time of his death. While the Jews were stoning him, he did not pay any attention to himself, but only remarked, "Lord, do not charge them with this sin" (Acts 7:60). His thoughts were on the others who were stoning him to death; he completely forgot about himself. He is not on the surface; he is a person who has entered into the surplus of grace.

As for the "water… deep enough to swim in—a river that no one could cross," it represents the love of God that is like an abundance of water, like a river that is too deep for swimming. Water one can swim in became a river that cannot be crossed— that has no end—the love of God. There is no end to the love of God, His mercy, or the work of His grace.

> He said to me, "Son of man, have you seen this?" Then he brought me and returned me to the bank of the river. When I returned, there, along the bank of the river, were very many trees on one side and the other. Then he said to me: "This water flows toward the eastern region, goes down into the valley, and enters the sea. When it reaches the sea, its waters are healed. And it shall be that every living thing that moves, wherever the rivers go, will live. There will be a very great multitude of fish, because these waters go there; for they will be healed, and everything will live wherever the river goes. It shall be that fishermen will stand by it from En Gedi to En Eglaim; they will be places for spreading their nets. Their fish will be of the same kinds as the fish of the Great Sea, exceedingly many." (Ezekiel 47:6–10)

What does this all mean? First, he saw many trees on the river of the grace of God. These are the faithful who are planted at the bank of the river; everything they do will *prosper*, according to the words of the first Psalm (1:3). Humans resemble trees bearing fruits throughout their life. If the trees represent the faithful, and fishermen stand with ready nets for the several kinds of fish to be caught, then what do the fish mean? Fish represent the sinners who are in the sea (of this turbulent world) and the water coming from the river to the sea represents the work of grace. God spoke concerning the water coming from the church to the sea—God's work of grace will reach the world. As we say in the doxology for the apostles, "Their voices went forth upon the face of all the earth, and their words have reached the ends of the world."

Reaching the sea, it will cure the water of the sea; God's grace will reach the world and change people—fish—sinners who have not yet learned to live in the good waters of the river, who continue to live in the sea of this world and its pleasures. Where the waters meet, where the water of God's grace touches the waters of the world, He will heal those souls it touches. Those sinners will repent and come to the church. These waters will revive a plethora of fish.

The fishermen stand ready to spread their nets; the fishermen (servants, priests, consecrates, and monastics) stand ready to serve and minister. As we say in the Psalmody, "You have chosen the publican and the adulteress You have saved." They are ready to catch the adulteress, the thief, the murderer, the tax collector, ones like St. Moses, St. Mary of Egypt, St. Paiesa, etc. There was truly a great catch; by the fourth century, Christianity had spread to the whole world.

> But its swamps and marshes will not be healed; they will be given over to salt. (Ezekiel 47:11)

Swamps and marshes originate from seas and are enclosed on themselves, representing the selfish self-sufficient people who are living for themselves, refusing to open up to the work of God's grace; that is why they will not be healed. Because of their selfishness, they will not bear fruits, "they will be given over to salt." God is glorified by everyone—by the saint and by the sinner (by Moses and by pharaoh)—including the swamps and marshes, which are enclosed on themselves and so are "given over to salt." Sea-salt is gathered from these salt-water marshes and swamps; God can extract something good even from the wicked.

> Along the bank of the river, on this side and that, will grow all kinds of trees used for food; their leaves will not wither, and their fruit will not fail. They will bear fruit every month, because their water flows from the sanctuary. Their fruit will be for food, and their leaves for medicine. (Ezekiel 47:12)

Let us talk about the leaves and the fruits. The leaves are the outward worship practices, such as attending church, fasting, praying, visiting the sick, and giving to the poor. The fruits are the inner essence. The truly faithful person bears both the leaves and the fruits of the Holy Spirit—not only the leaves without the fruits (as in the case of the cursed fig tree)—so that they, through true faith, are full of the fruits of the Holy Spirit, but also of the leaves.

If, in my service or my monastic life, I am attending liturgies, praises, living according to my spiritual canon, but have no fruits, I will be like the fig tree from which the Lord Christ sought fruit but found none. The true monastic, the consecrated, the bishop, clergy, and all servants should have a life that reflects the outward signs of worship, but they should also bear fruits—the fruits of Christ.

Another point about the leaves and fruits: "Their fruit will be for food, and their leaves for medicine." What does this mean? *Fruit for food* means we nourish others, either through our charity or by offering them love, bearing with them, sharing in their happiness, empowering them, and being long-suffering with them. For this reason, everyone who deals with a believer will be satiated.

Why are the "leaves for medicine"? If we do not have leaves (do not attend church, do not partake of Communion, do not attend the Midnight Praises, do not attend Vespers), then we are a stumbling block for others—the absence of leaves creates obstacles for others. The presence of leaves protects against this offense. The leaves also heal because they provide a good role model to others. The leaves of outer worship function as a prophylactic against offenses and as a medicine by role modeling.

Here ends the vision of the water.

Glory be to God forever. Amen.

www.ingramcontent.com/pod-product-compliance
Lightning Source LLC
Chambersburg PA
CBHW060412050426
42449CB00009B/1960